FUNDRUM MY CONUNDRUM

BY

BEN KOVLER AND RAY EPSTEIN

EDITED BY GAIL EPSTEIN KOVLER

ILLUSTRATED BY SHELLY KOVLER

FUNDRUM PUBLISHING
CHICAGO

Cover art by Eric Luden

fundrum

repstein@fundrum.com
www.fundrum.com

These puzzles have been in our family for many years and have occupied our minds at the dinner table and in the swimming pool. We have tried to work them out in many ways and with many different people. But the person who gave these riddles to us first was my grandfather, Raymond Epstein. I would implore him to ask me more riddles and every time he was able to come up with one just harder than the one I had solved a minute before. The answers sometimes came easy and sometimes took two to three weeks. During the thinking time I would ask for the answer, but with a firm smile, Grandpa would tell me to think a little longer. And, sure enough, after a little more thought, the answer would present itself in my mind.

I hope you can get the fun and satisfaction out of these riddles that I have. I would like to thank my Grandpa for all the time that he has taken to help me, talk to me, or even just be there for me when I needed him. So I hope that you will get a kick out of these puzzles and remember, ***Fundrum My Conundrum***.

Ben Kovler
Oct. '92
Age 14

Although these brain-teasers are primarily intended for youngsters, we note that a surprising number of adults enjoy the challenge they present. Moreover, many of them have found as I did, hours of companionship with their children and grandchildren. And so it goes, from generation to generation.

For me, my delight in Ben's quick wit, in my daughter Gail's capacity for seeing the project through, and in sharing puzzle sessions with grandchildren Molly, Alex, and Rachel has been an extraordinary pleasure.

Happy solving!

Ray Epstein
Oct. '92
Age 74

Novice Puzzles

1

A big Indian and a little Indian are walking down the street. The little Indian is the **son** of the big Indian but the big Indian is **not** the father of the little Indian. *How is this possible?*

Answer on page 101

2

What is in seasons, seconds, centuries and minutes but not in decades, years or days?

Answer on page 10

3

One cigarette can be made from four butts (stubs). If a man has 16 cigarettes, *how many cigarettes can he smoke?*

SURGEON GENERAL'S WARNING: Smoking Causes Lung Cancer, Heart Disease, Emphysema, And May Complicate Pregnancy.

Answer on page 102

4

All amoebas duplicate
themselves every minute
An amoeba which does so is placed
in a jar at exactly ten o'clock in the morning
At 12:00 noon the jar is full
At what time is the jar half full

Answer on page 103

5

A prisoner is told "If you tell a lie we will hang you; if you tell the truth we will shoot you." *What statement can he make about the situation to save himself?*

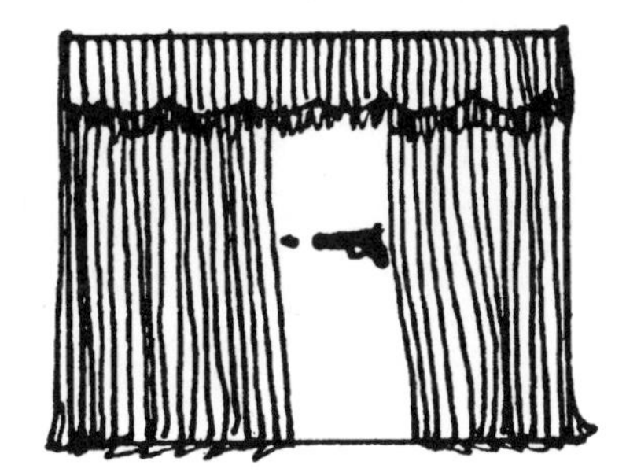

Answer on page 104

6

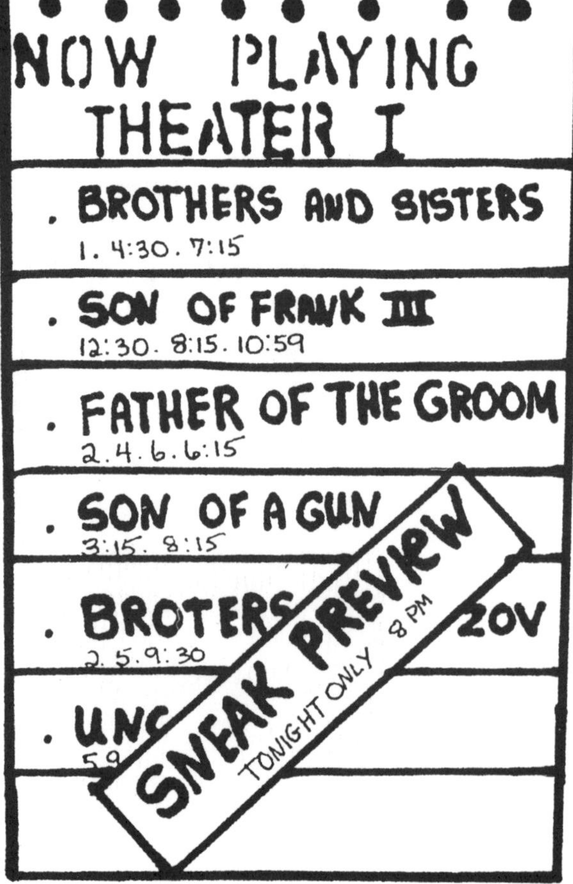

Looking at a picture a man says "Brothers and sisters I have none but that man's father is my father's son." *Whose picture is it?*

Answer on page 106

7

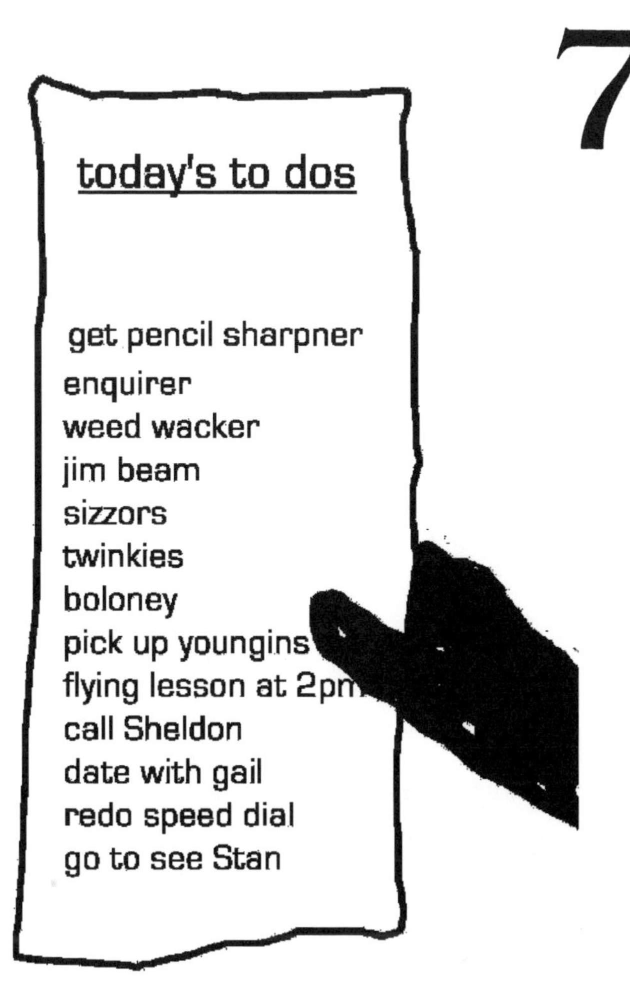

A person who was unable to hear or speak entered a store to buy a wall pencil sharpener. To make the clerk understand what he wanted, he poked a finger into his left ear and then made a grinding motion around his other ear with his fist. The clerk understood at once. A man who was unable to see now entered the store. *How did he make the clerk understand that he wanted to buy a pair of scissors?*

Answer on page 107

I have two coins making 55 cents but one is not a nickel. *How can that be?*

Answer on page 1

9

The two sons of an arab sheik were each overwhelmingly proud of their own horse. When the sheik died he left instructions that they have a race and the one whose horse **loses** the race would inherit his fortune. They started to race at full speed but gradually slowed down and stopped, not knowing what to do.

A passing traveler heard their story and advised them whereupon they jumped on the horses and raced as fast as they could to the finish line. *What was the advice?*

Answer on page 109

10

What is the next number in this sequence - 77,49,36,18?

Answer on page 10

11

Why are 1977 dollars worth more than 1976 dollars?

Answer on page 101

12

An American man marries 20 women. They are now all alive; there have been no divorces; he is not a polygamist and has done nothing illega

How can this be?

Answer on page

13

What is the eleven letter word that all Yale graduates spell incorrectly?

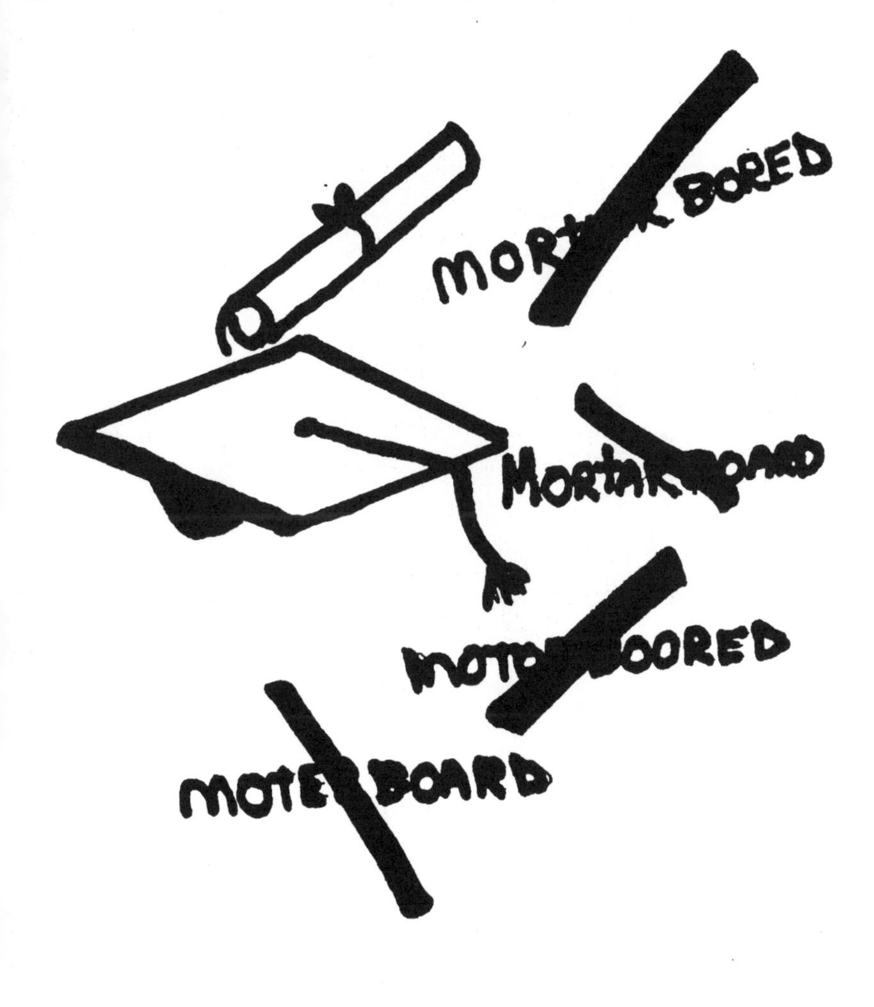

Answer on page 103

14

A clock strikes the hour on the hour, and once at the quarter, half and three-quarters of the hour. *How is it possible to hear 1 chime, 9 times in a row at 15 minute intervals?*

Answer on page 1

15

If someone finds an old coin bearing the date 47 BC and offers to sell it to you for one dollar - *is it a good buy?*

Answer on page 106

16

In Illinois is it legal for a man to marry his widow's sister?

Answer on page 10

17

How much dirt is there in a hole that measures two feet by three feet by four feet?

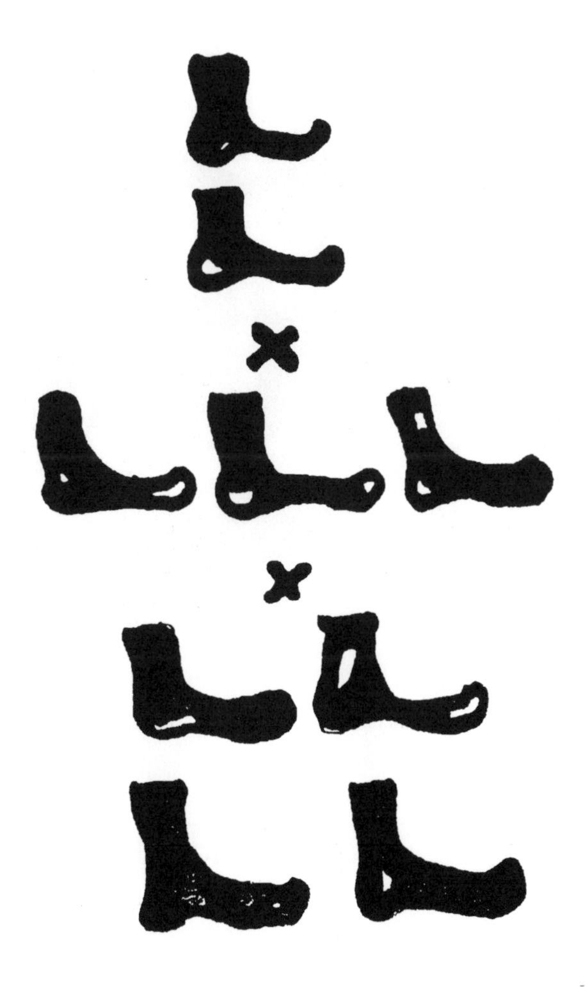

Answer on page 108

18

How many months have 30 days in them?

Answer on page 1(

19

A shepherd had 17 sheep. All but nine died. *How many did he have left?*

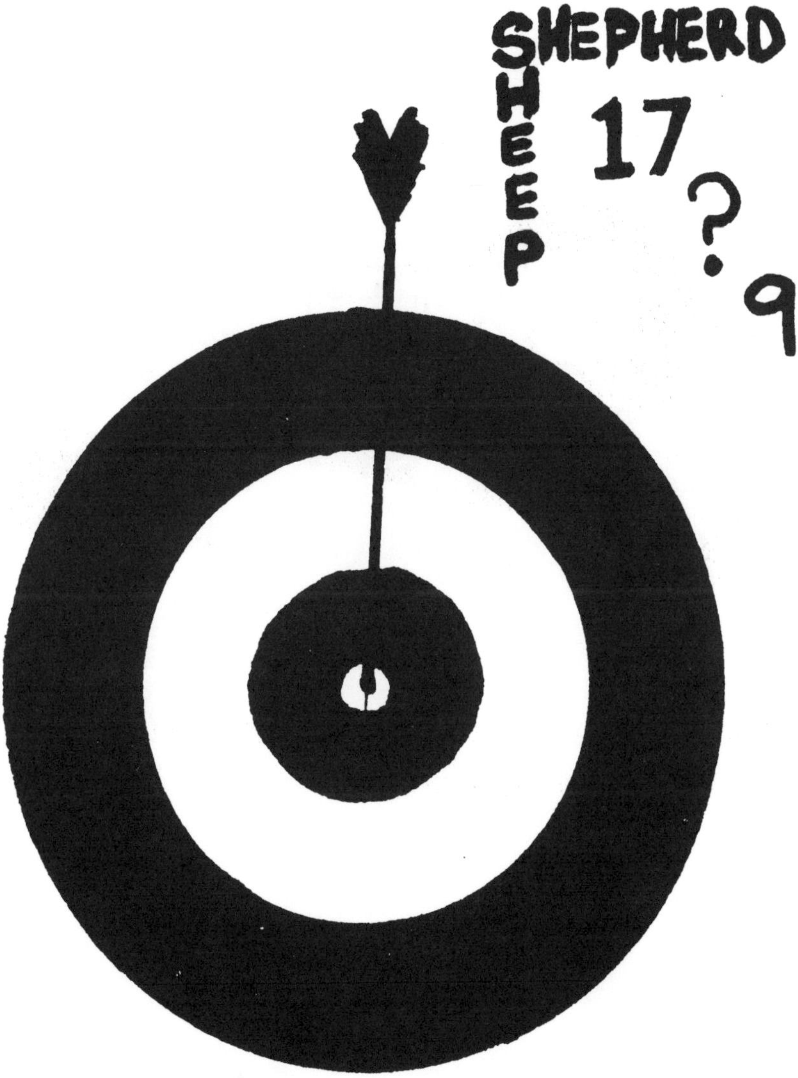

Answer on page 109

20

Which is correct - eight and eight **is** fifteen or eight and eight **are** fifteen?

Answer on page 10

21

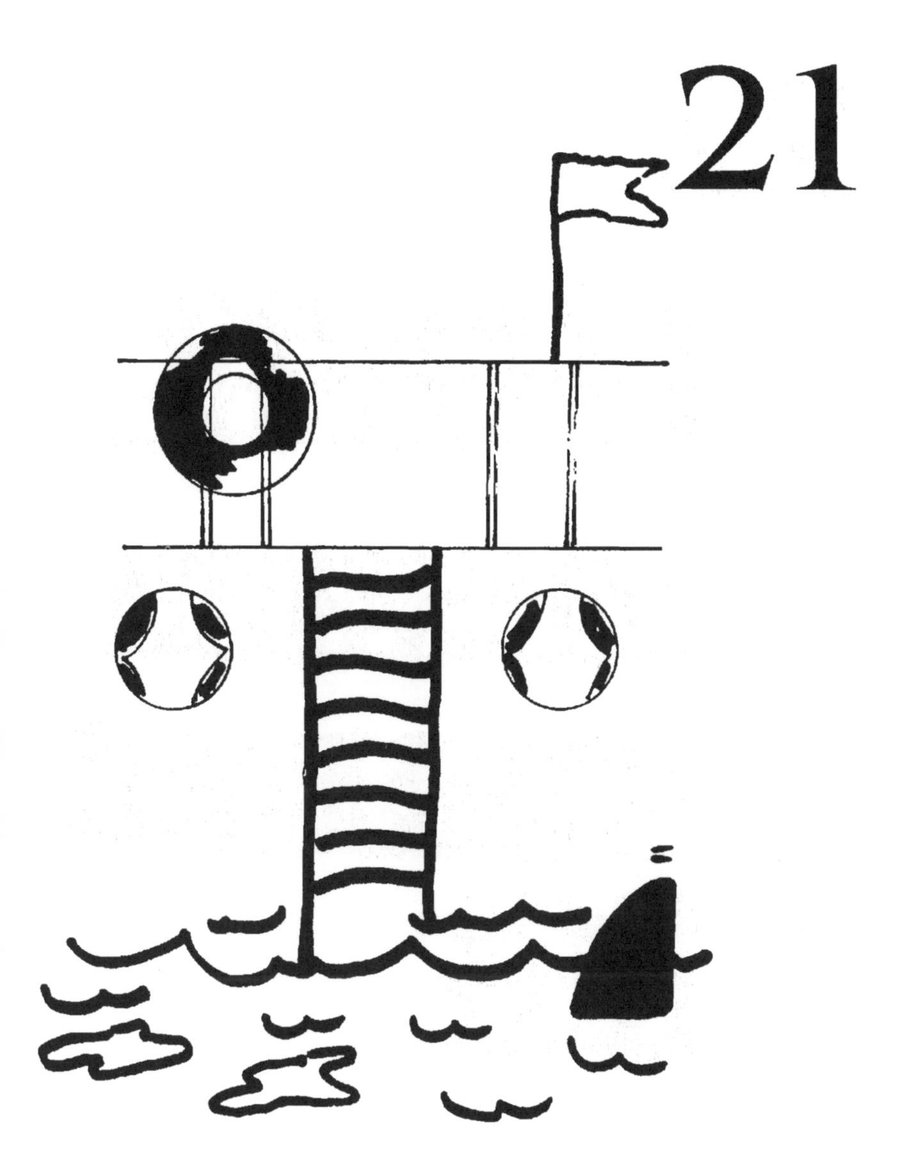

A 10 foot rope ladder hangs over the side of a boat with the bottom rung just barely covered by the surface of the water. There is one foot between rungs and the tide goes up at the rate of 6 inches per hour. *How long until three rungs are covered?*

Answer on page 101

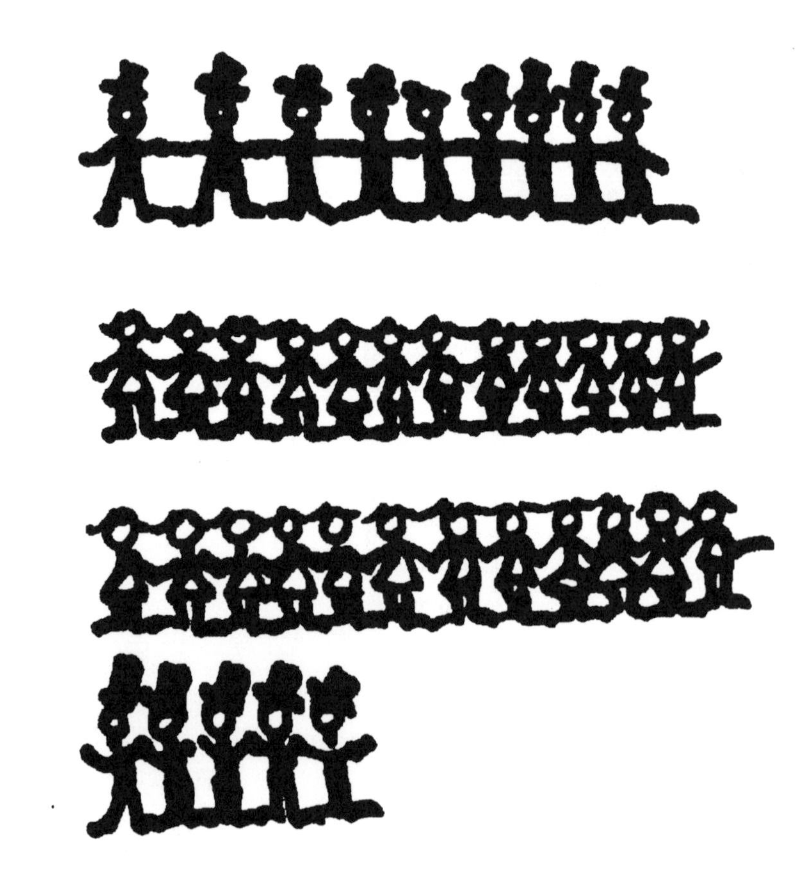

Mr. and Mrs. Smith have six daughters and each daughter has a brother. *How many people are in the family?*

Answer on page 103

23

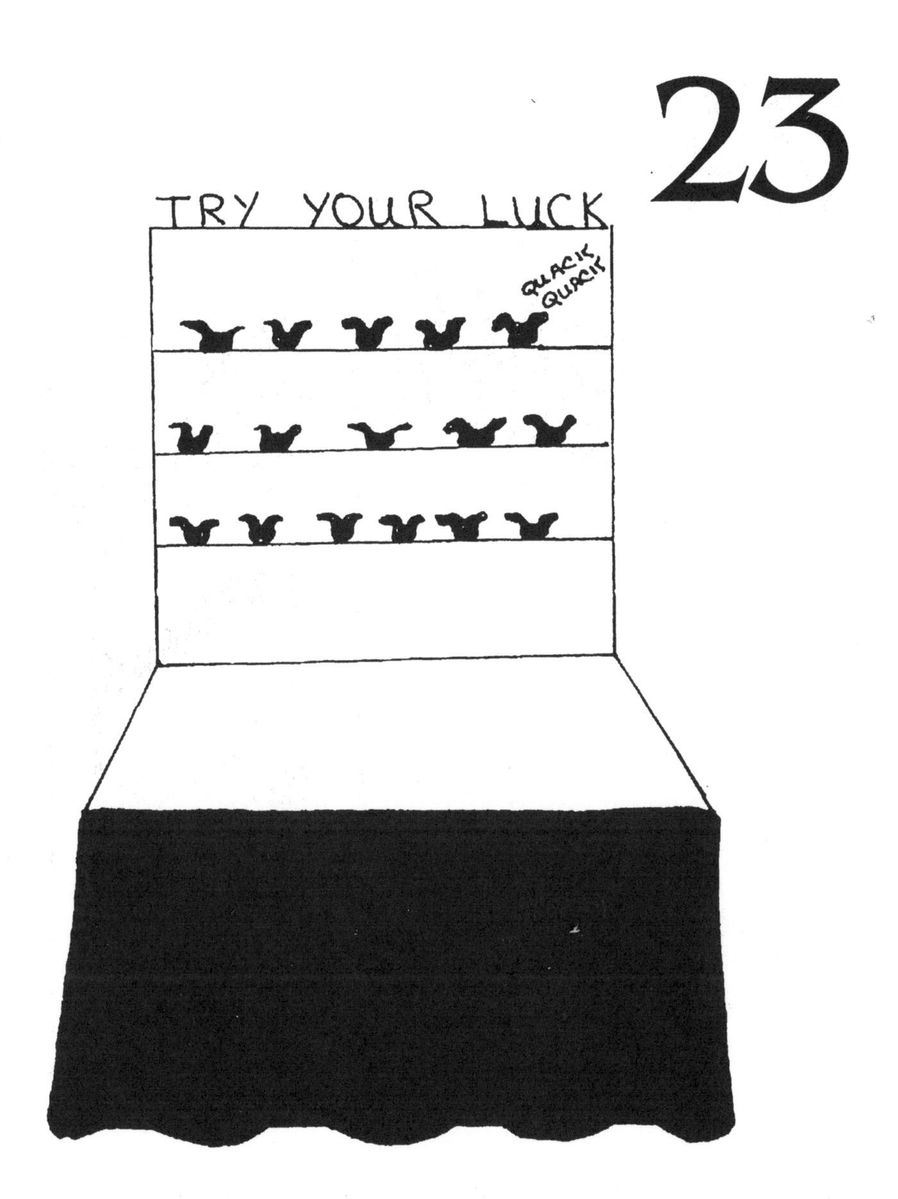

Two fathers and two sons each shot a duck and none of them shot the same duck. Only three ducks were shot. *Why?*

Answer on page 103

24

We all know there are 12 one-cent stamps in a dozen, *but how many two-cent stamps are there in a dozen?*

Answer on page 104

25

Read the following out loud, quickly!

PARIS
IN THE
THE SPRING

Answer on page 106

How long will an eight-day clock run without winding?

Answer on page 1

27

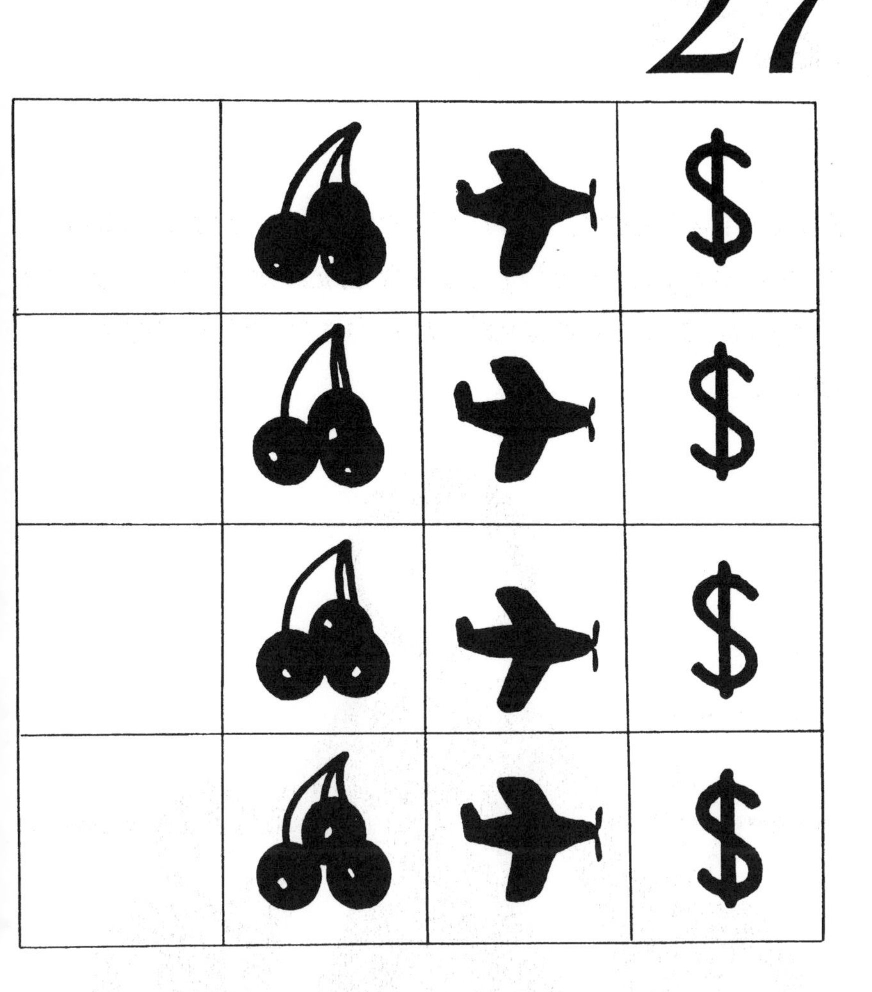

Two planes leave Chicago and New York at the same time. Assume a 1000 mile distance between them. The east bound plane travels 240 miles per hour but due to headwinds the west bound plane can only make 80 miles per hour. *When they meet, which is nearest to Chicago?*

Answer on page 108

A boat will carry only 200 pounds. *How can a man weighing 200 pounds and his 2 sons, each weighing 100 pounds, use the boat to cross a river?*

Answer on page 109

A bottle and a cork together cost \$105. The bottle costs \$100 more than the cork.
How much does each cost?

Answer on page 111

Take 2 apples from 3 apples
and what have you got?

Answer on page 101

31

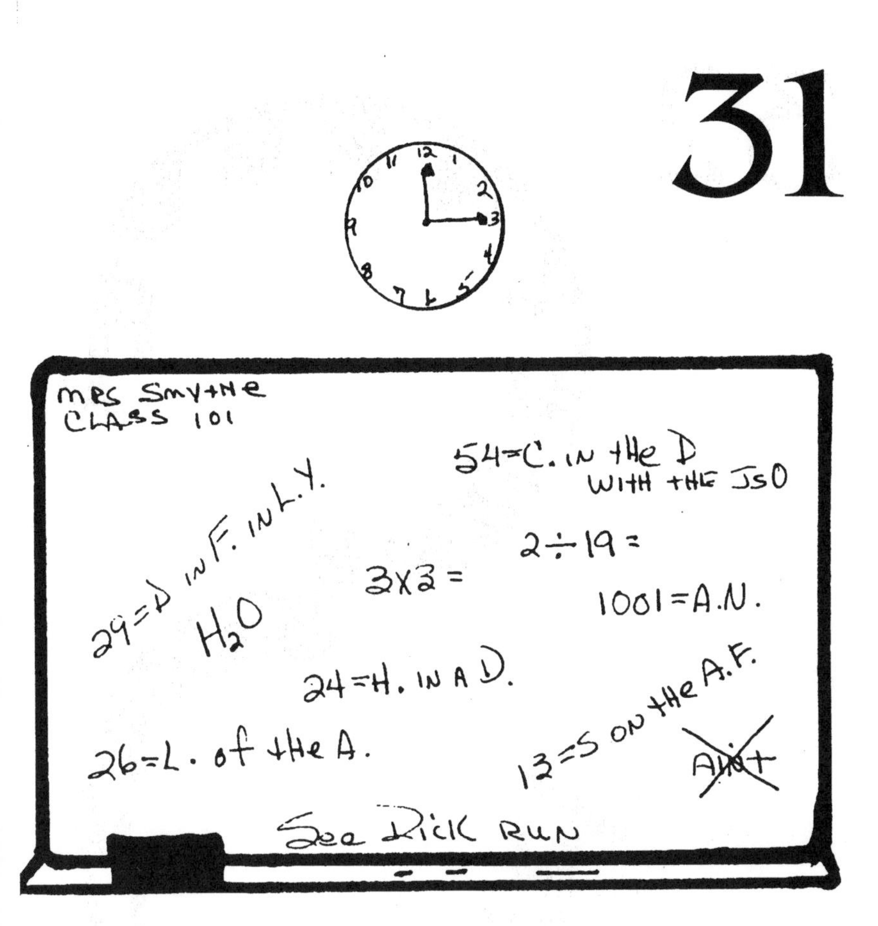

What do the following represent:

A. 1001=A.N.

B. 54=C. in the D. (with the Js)

C. 29=D. in F. in L.Y.

D. 24=H. in a D.

E. 13=S. on the A.F.

F. 26=L. of the A.

Answer on page 102

32

In English, to the end of what plural noun can you add an S and make it a singular noun?

Answer on page 103

There are three errers in the statement of this problem. You must detect all of them to recieve full credit.

Answer on page 104

A King wanted to get rid of his Prime Minister so he told three judges that he would put two slips of paper in a hat and have the Prime Minister draw one of them to decide his fate.

He said that one slip would be marked "GO" and the other "STAY." But the King cheated and marked both of them "GO." The Prime Minister suspected that the King would cheat and planned accordingly. *After drawing one slip, what did the Prime Minister say to the judges that forced the King to let him stay?*

Answer on page 104

Medium Puzzles

In three boxes we have one containing 2 black marbles, one with 2 white marbles and one with a black and a white. The boxes are all labeled **incorrectly**. *How many times must you pick a single marble blindly out of a box to correctly identify what each box contains?*

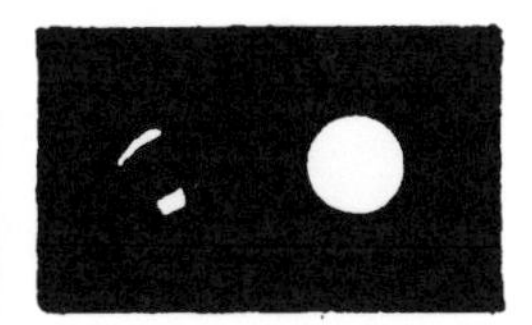

Answer on page 106

36

A single elimination tennis tournament starts with a certain number of players. *How many matches must be played until a winner is arrived at in a tournament*

a) with 100 players?
b) with 1,500 players?
c) with 147,690 players?

Answer on page 107

You have 12 black sox and 12 white sox mixed up in a drawer. *What is the least number of sox you can pull out – blindly – to be sure of getting a matching pair?*

Answer on page 108

A barbecue grill holds two steaks at a time. It takes ten minutes to grill one side of a steak. *What is the minimum amount of time it would take to grill three steaks on both sides?*

Answer on page 109

A gold bar is notched into 7 segments. A traveler with this bar arrives at a hotel wishing to stay for 7 days. The charge at the hotel is one segment per night to be paid daily. *What is the fewest number of times the traveler must cut the bar so that one segment is paid every day?*

Answer on page 111

40

You have five pieces of chain each consisting of three links. It costs 25 cents to open one link and weld it closed again. *What is the minimum it would cost to make one straight chain, 15 links long?*

Answer on page 1

41

Coins are supposed to weigh one ounce. Among 100 bags, each of which contains 100 coins, one contains coins weighing only 3/4 of an ounce. In one weighing on a digital scale, *how can you determine the bag with the bad coins?*

Answer on page 102

42

Villains always lie, good guys always tell the truth You see three men on the road and you ask the first one "What are you, villain or a good guy?" You cannot make out his mumble answer so you ask the second man "What did he say?" The second man replies "He said he is a villain." The third man says "The second man is lying." *Is the third ma a villain or a good guy?*

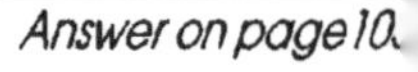
Answer on page 10

43

'wo trains are 100 miles apart, approaching each other. One train goes 50 miles per hour and the other 25 miles per hour. A bird flies back and forth between the two trains at a speed of 75 miles per hour. *How far has the bird flown when the trains meet?*

Answer on page 104

Complete these sequences of letters. O.T.T.F.F. — M.T.W.T. — D.N.O.S.A.

Answer on page 105

45

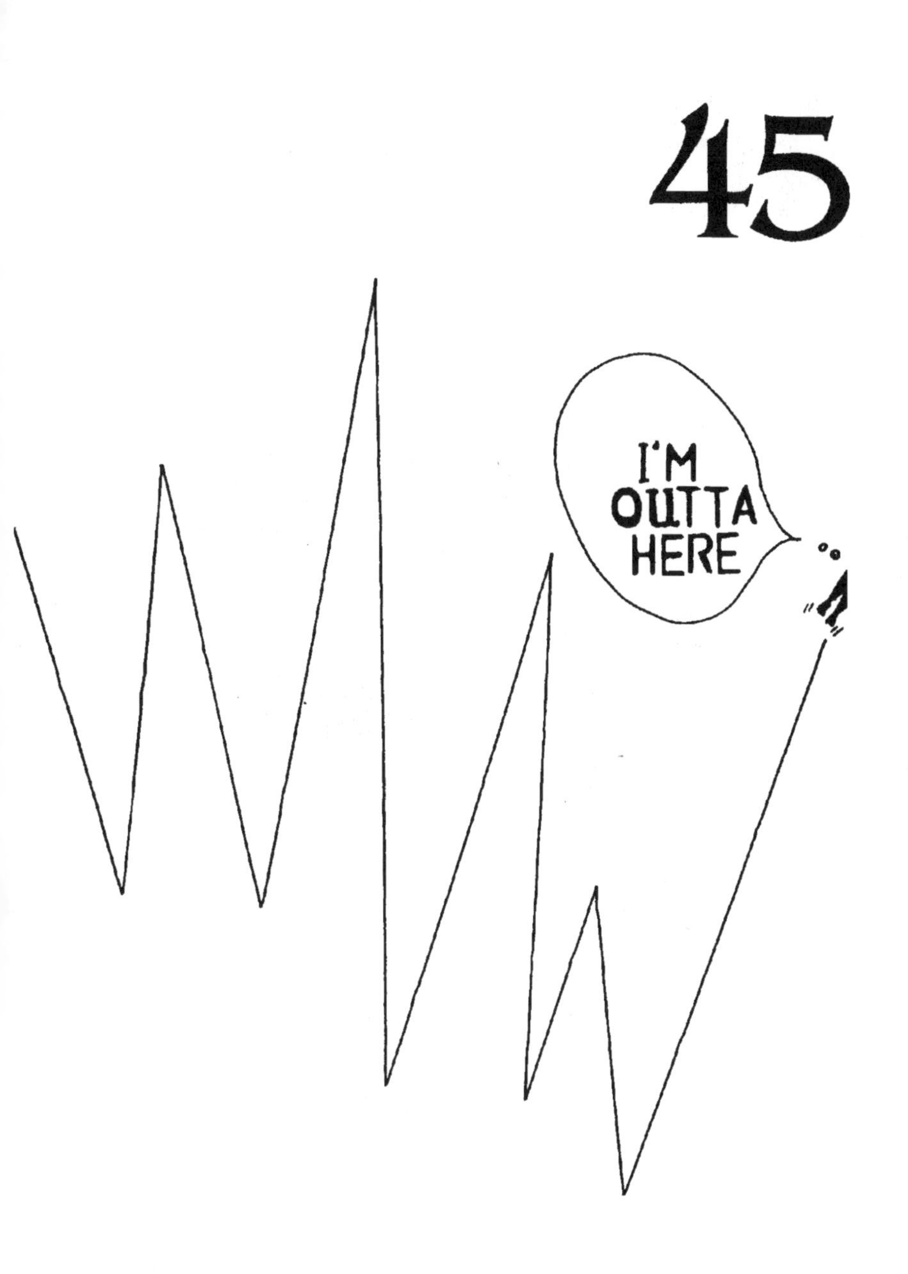

A frog in a well 20 feet deep jumps up 5 feet each day but falls back 4 feet after hitting the wall. *How many days until he gets out?*

Answer on page 106

46

On a 12 hour analog clock, how many times does the minute hand pass the hour hand between one minute after noon and one minute before midnight on the same day?

Answer on page 107

47

A woman with no driver's license goes the wrong way on a one-way street and turns left at a corner with a no left turn sign. A policeman sees her but does nothing. *Why?*

Answer on page 108

Three men have a duel to the death. They have varying degrees of skill. Alex hits his desired target 3 times out of 3; Max hits his 2 times out of 3; Jake hits his 1 time out of 3. Jake goes first. *What is the optimal thing for him to do?*

Answer on page 110

How many nines are there counting from 1 to 100?

Answer on page111

50

Which one of the following doesn't belong in this group? Uncle, cousin, mother, sister, father, aunt.

Answer on page 10

51

A hill is a mile up and a mile down. If you drive up the hill at 30 miles per hour, *how fast must you come down to average 60 miles per hour for the whole hill?*

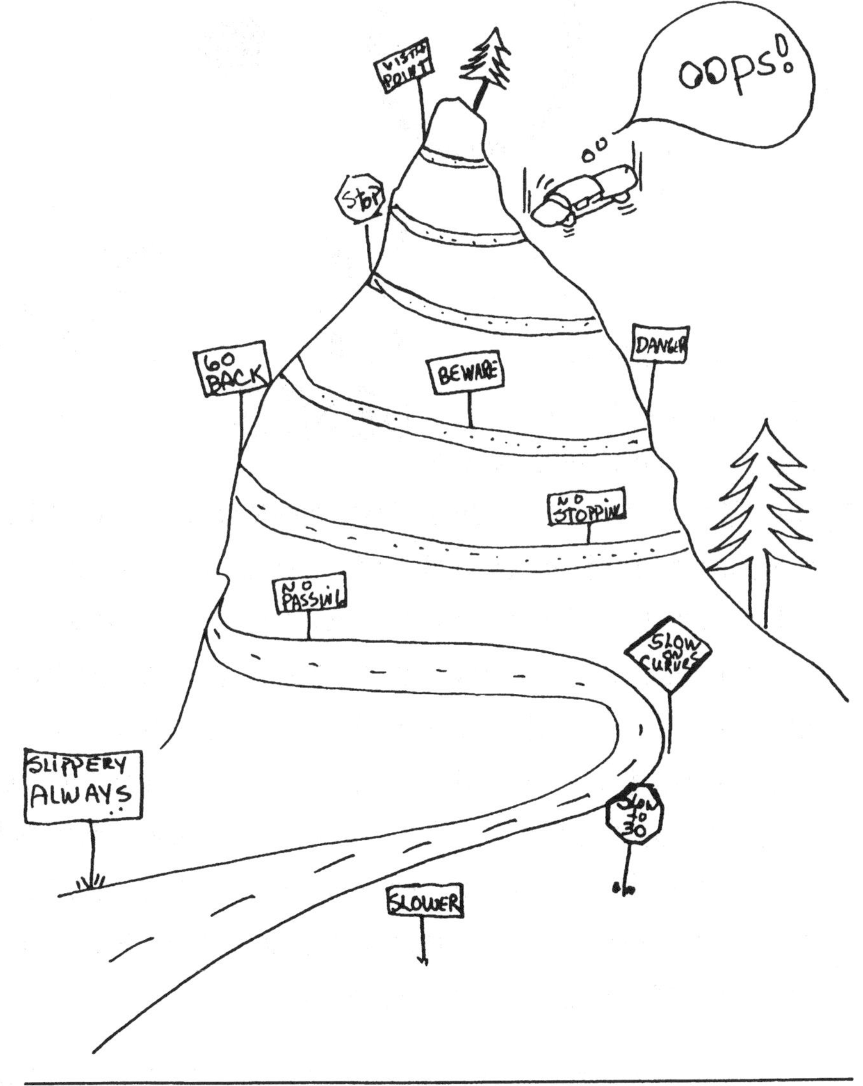

Answer on page 102

52

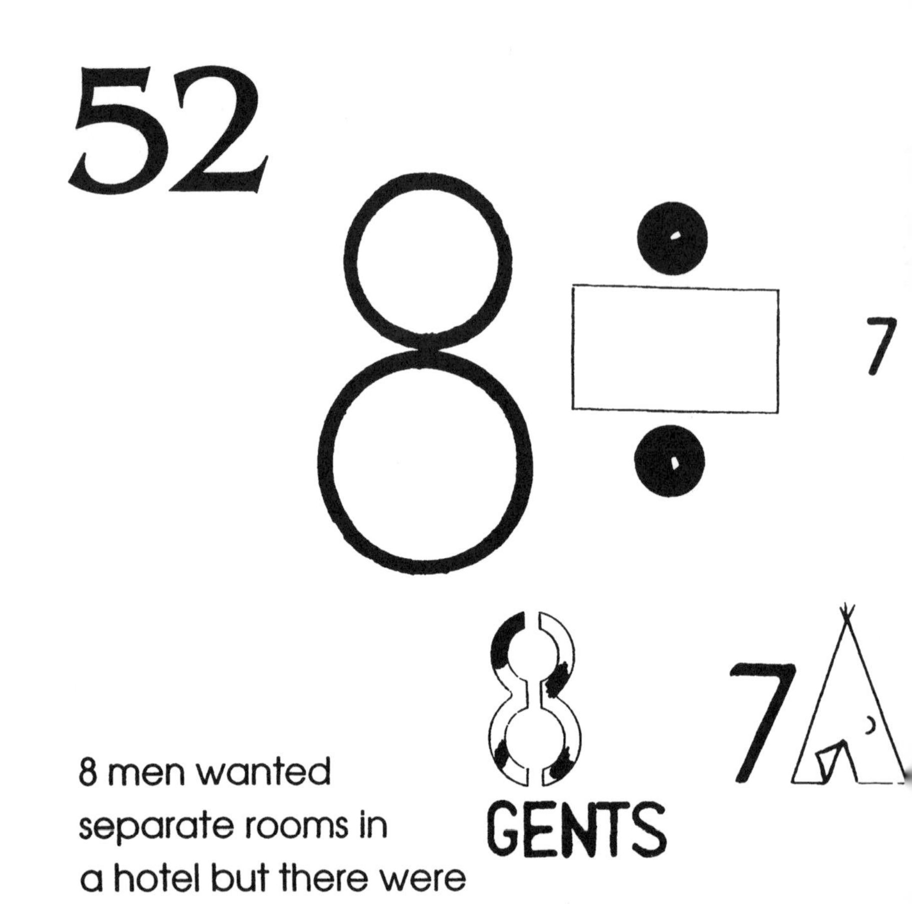

8 men wanted separate rooms in a hotel but there were only 7 rooms available. The clerk said he could handle it and proceeded to put 2 men in the 1st room, the third man in the 2nd room, the fourth man in the 3rd room, the fifth man in the 4th room, the sixth man in the 5th room, and the seventh man in the 6th room. He now took one of the men out of the 1st room and placed him in the last, the 7th, room. So he managed to put 8 men in 7 rooms with each one having a separate room. *Did he really?*

Answer on page 103

In a certain downtown building, Everett likes daffodils but not roses; Shelly likes zucchini but not cucumbers; Bill likes vanilla but not chocolate; Harriet likes books but not movies. Peter, the building engineer, can't figure out what's going on, *can you?*

Answer on page 104

54

You have a fox, a chicken and a sack of grain. You must cross a river with only one of them at a time. If you leave the fox with the chicken he will eat it; if you leave the chicken with the grain he will eat it. *How can you get all three across safely?*

Answer on page 105

55

A three volume set of books stands on the bookshelf. Each cover is 1/4 of an inch thick and the sum of the pages of each book is 1 inch. A bookworm starts on page 1 of Volume 1 and eats his way to the last page of Volume 3. *How far does he travel?*

Answer on page 106

56

Three travelers register at a hotel and are told that their rooms will cost $10 each so they pay $30. Later the clerk realizes that he made a mistake and should only have charged them $25. He gives a bellboy $5 to return to them but the bellboy is dishonest and gives each of them only $1, keeping $2 for himself. So the men actually spent $27 and the bellboy kept $2: *what happened to the other dollar of the original $30?*

Answer on page 107

Meeting two people and not knowing whether they are good guys (who always tell the truth) or villains (who always lie) we ask the first one if he is a truth teller. We cannot make out his mumbled answer but the second man tells us "He said yes, but he's a big liar." *What are they?*

Answer on page 108

GRASSHOPPER

If a grasshopper halves the distance to a wall on every jump, *how many jumps will he need to reach the wall if he starts from ten feet away?*

Answer on page 110

59

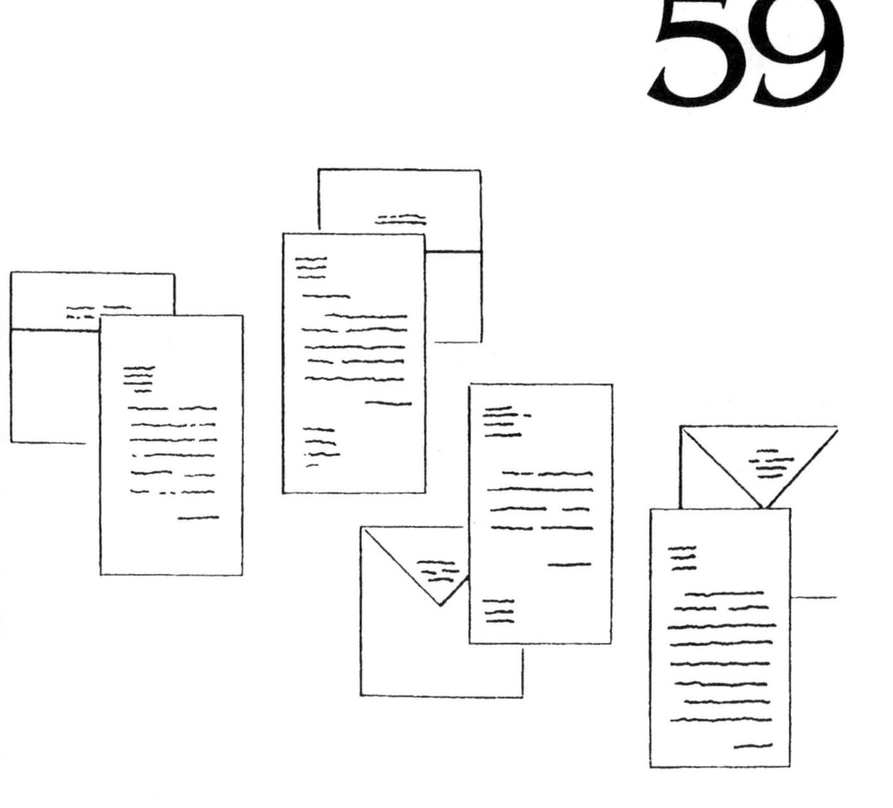

A secretary types four letters to four different people and addresses four envelopes. She puts the letters into the envelopes at random without looking. *What are the chances that exactly three letters will be in the correct envelopes?*

Answer on page 111

Can you draw four straight lines without lifting your pencil from the paper that will go thru each dot once?

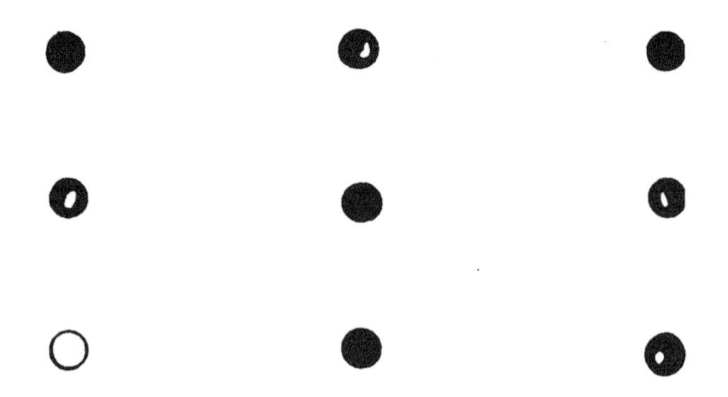

Answer on page 101

61

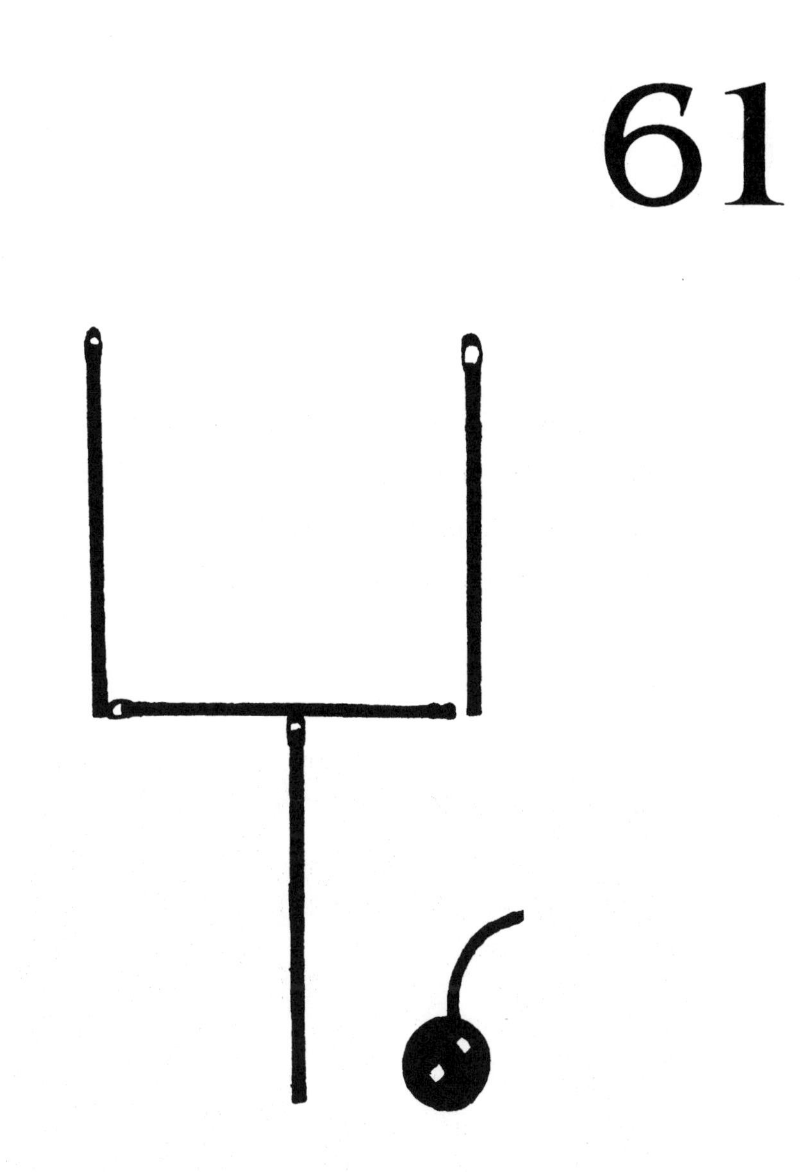

Can you move two matches and end up with the cherry in the cocktail glass?

Answer on page 102

62

Can you place eight pieces on a checkerboard so that no two are on the same line vertically, horizontally or diagonally?

Answer on page 103

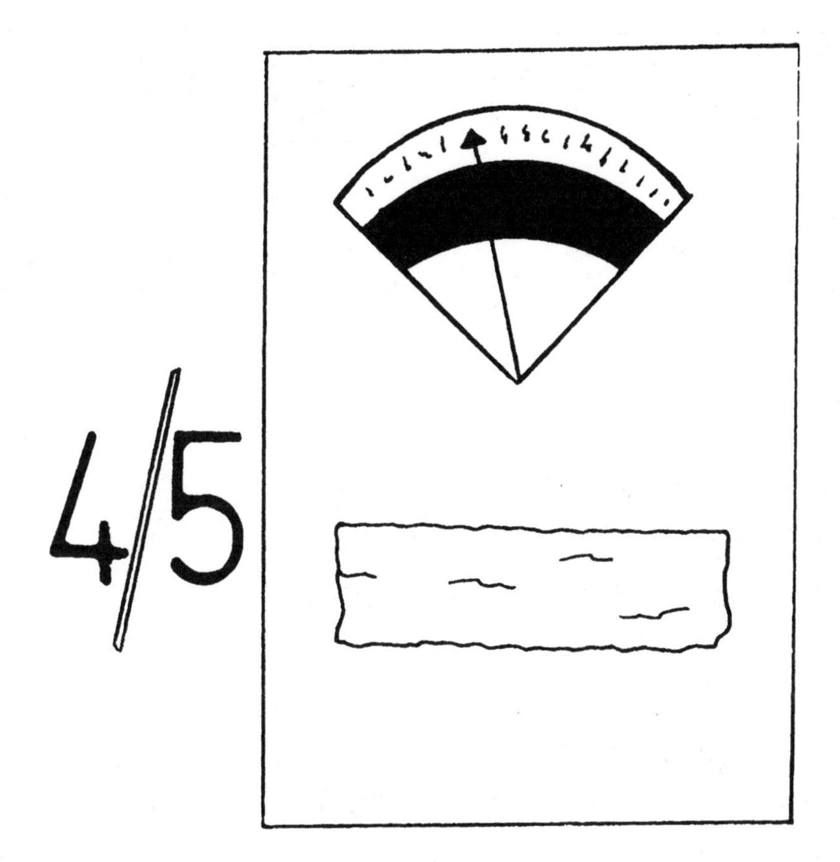

A brick weighs $^4/_5$ of its weight plus $^4/_5$ of a pound. *How much does it weigh?*

Answer on page 104

64

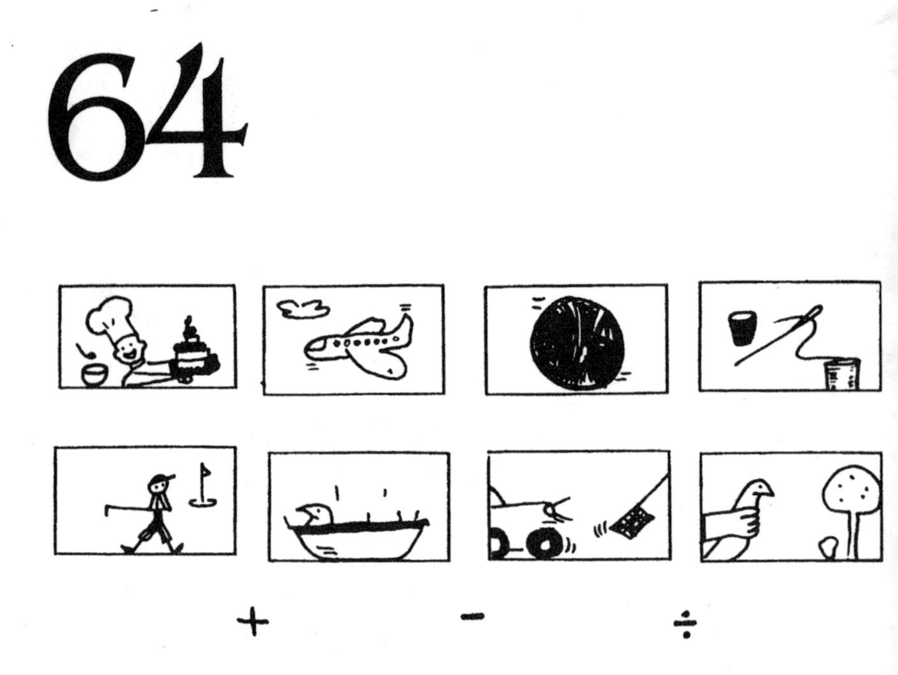

ADD a baker's dozen, the number of the Boeing superjet, baseball's "stretch" inning, the number saved by a stitch in time, what a golfer yells before hitting a long shot.

SUBTRACT the number of blackbirds baked in a pie, and the number of miles driven in the Indianapolis Memorial Race.

DIVIDE by the number of birds in the hand that one in the bush is worth.

What do you get?

Answer on page 105

65

Three men each charged a different price per hour for their services. Using the grid below can you *identify each person's full name, his profession and his price?*

1. The Professor charged the least.
2. Ben was not the lawyer.
3. Ray charged less than Jones who did not use the doctor.
4. Smith charged $15.

	Smith	Jones	Brown	Lawyer	Doctor	Professor	$5	$10	$15
Ray									
Gail									
Ben									
$5									
$10									
$15									
Lawyer									
Doctor									
Professor									

Answer on page 107

66

A man bet that there would be at least seven total runs scored in a certain baseball game. In the bottom of the 9th inning the score was 3 to 2 with no one on base. A batter is at the plate and one pitch is made. After the play, the man says, "I've won!" and leaves. *How did he know for sure that he had won his bet?*

Answer on page 10

67

Here are some sentences in which the names of countries are hidden. See if you can find them by joining two adjacent words or parts of words:

1. The health spa in the travel folder looked attractive.
2. Water was rationed so each got a small can a day.
3. Elvira questioned the monthly electric bill.
4. Swollen glands can be very painful.
5. We had to wait for supper until the guests arrived.
6. Shout, "Hail," and be recognized.
7. You're a Roman, I assume.
8. Yes, we deny all of the charges, judge.

Answer on page 108

Hard Puzzles

8 BBs look alike but one is slightly heavier than the others. *How can you identify the heavy BB in only two weighings on a balance scale?*

Answer on page 110

A man has an office north of his home and a factory south of his home. Every day he goes to the train platform at completely random, different times. There is a train going north, stopping on one side of the platform, every ten minutes. There is a train going south, stopping on the other side of the same platform, every ten minutes. He always takes the first train that comes along after his arrival on the platform. Nine days out of ten he goes to his office.

Why?

Answer on page 111

70

A man leaves home, makes three left turns and comes home to find two masked men there.
What is this all about?

Answer on page 101

71

A man drives 10,000 miles in his car. He changes his tires around so that all 5 (including the spare) get an equal number of miles of wear. *How many miles does each tire get?*

Answer on page 102

72

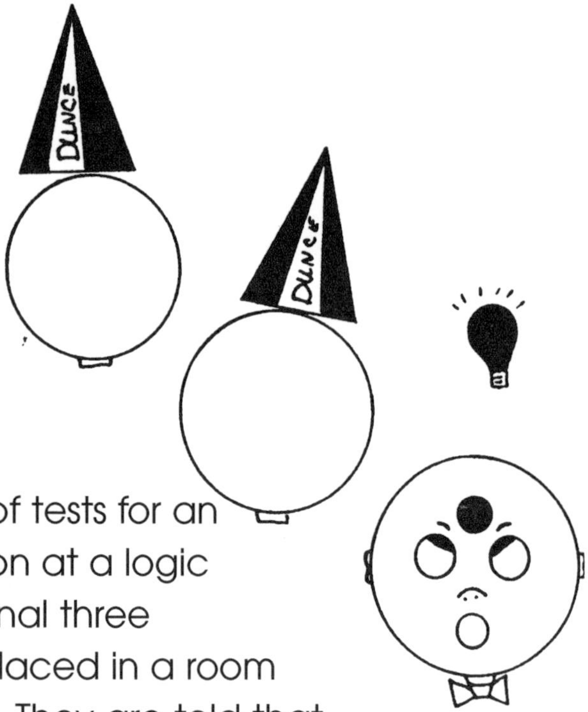

After a number of tests for an esteemed position at a logic based firm, the final three applicants are placed in a room and blindfolded. They are told that a mark, either black or white, is being placed on each forehead. After the blindfolds have been removed, they are asked to raise a hand if they see a black mark on either of the other two applicants' foreheads. Unbeknownst to the applicants, black marks are placed on all three foreheads and, of course, when the blindfolds are removed, they all raise their hands. They are told that whoever first figures out what is on his or her forehead will get the job. After a little while, one announces that he is sure he has a black mark. *How did he know for sure?*

Answer on page 103

73

A square window, 4 feet by 4 feet, is to have half of one side of its surface painted black but still leave a transparent square measuring 4 feet up and down and 4 feet side to side (the window is two-dimensional). *How can this feat be accomplished?*

Answer on page 104

74

A man enters a town having only two barber shops and wants a haircut. He sees that in one shop it is neat and clean and the barber has a very nice haircut. In the other, the shop is messy with hair all over the floor and the barber has a bad haircut. He chooses to go to the messy one. *Why?*

Answer on page 105

75

Quickly give 100 words with no "a" in them.

Answer on page 107

76

You have two hourglasses - one measures 7 minutes and one measures 4 minutes. *How can you time 9 minutes?*

Answer on page 107

77

Mr. A lies on Mondays, Tuesdays and Wednesdays; Mr. B lies on Thursdays, Fridays and Saturdays. One day Mr. A said "Yesterday was one of my lying days." Mr. B said "Yesterday was one of my lying days too."
What day of the week was it?

Answer on page 109

78

A rope takes one hour to burn from one end to the other. It does not burn at a constant rate. You have two such ropes and need to measure exactly 45 minutes. *How can you do so?*

Answer on page110

79

We meet three people and don't know if they are good guys (who always tell the truth) or villains (who always lie). #1 says "All of us are villains." #2 says "Exactly one of us is a good guy." *What are each of the three?*

Answer on page 111

80

The length of a certain fish is equal to 20 plus $^1/_2$ its length. The head of the fish is 9 inches; the body is equal to the head plus the tail. *How long is the body? The tail?*

Answer on page 101

81

A man can perform a certain task in three days working alone. He has a helper who takes two days to do what the first man can do in one. *How long will it take to get the task done if they both do it together?*

Answer on page 102

Can you name ten body parts containing only three letters each?

Answer on page 103

83

A town has 20,000 people in it.
5% of them are one-legged and one half of the other people go barefoot.
How many shoes are needed?

Answer on page 104

84

The Smiths have a number of birdhouses in their yard and all are occupied. Since there are more birdhouses than there are birds in any one house, at least two of the birdhouses must contain the same number of birds. *True?*

Answer on page 105

The following diagram shows a railroad switch. A and B are boxcars and E is an engine which is larger than the boxcars. The piece of track from X to Y is long enough to accept a boxcar but not long enough for the engine. *How can you push and pull to switch the two boxcars?*

Answer on page 107

86

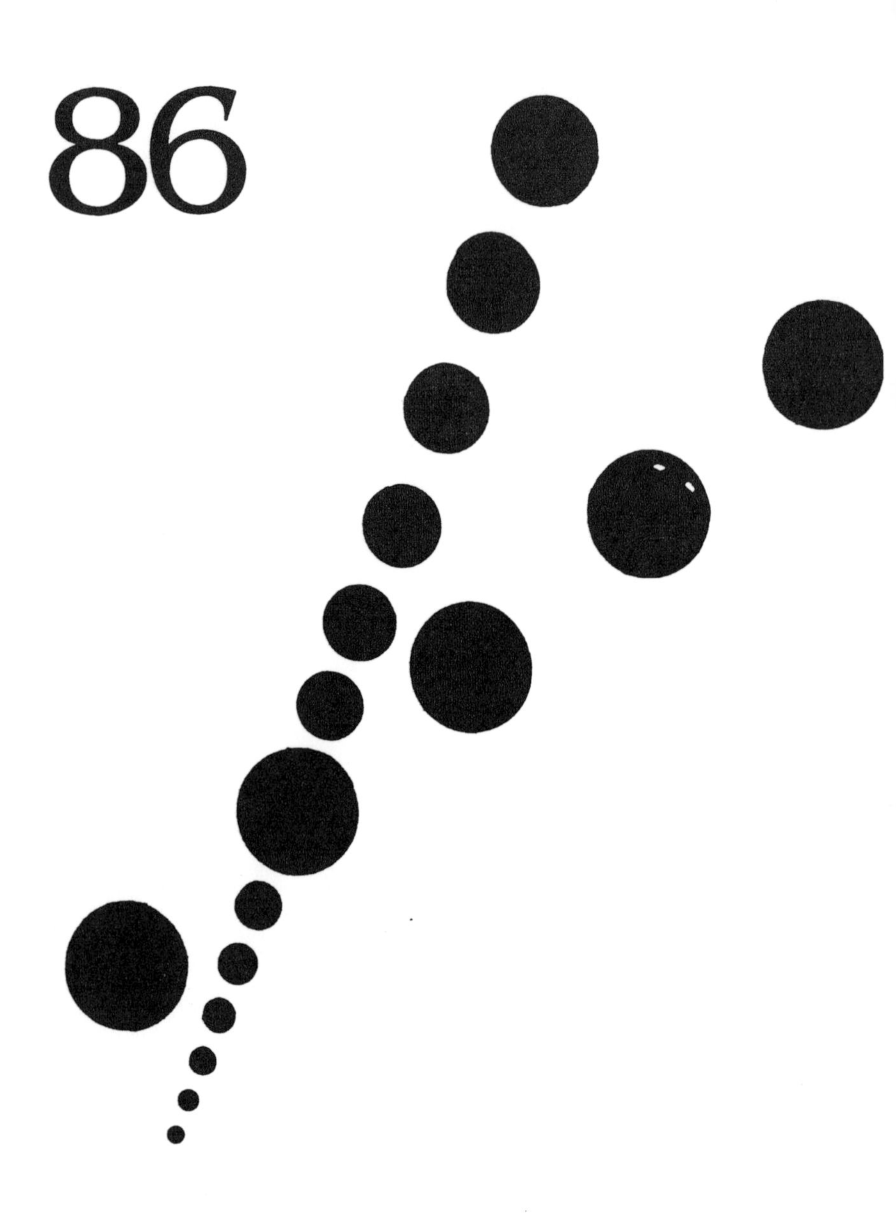

How can you throw a ball and make it stop and come back to you without it touching anything or having anything attached to it?

Answer on page 108

87

A group of airplanes is based on a small island. The tank of each plane holds just enough fuel to take it half way around the world. Fuel can be transferred from the tank of one plane to the tank of another while in flight. The only source of fuel is on the island and there is no time lost in refueling either in the air or on the ground. All planes have the same constant ground speed and rate of fuel consumption. All planes return safely to the island. *What is the smallest number of planes that will ensure the flight of one plane all the way around the world on a great circle?*

Answer on page 109

88

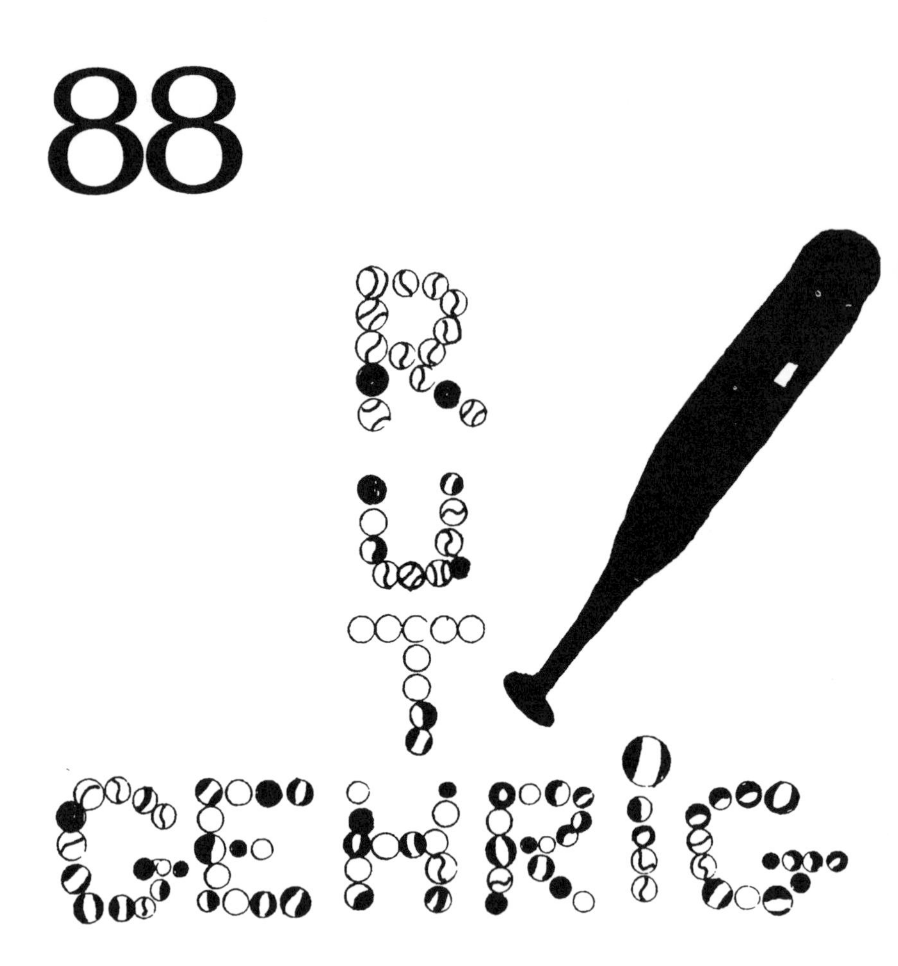

During a certain baseball season Babe Ruth had a higher batting average than Lou Gehrig for the first half of the season—and again the Babe fared better at the plate than Lou in the second half of the season. **However**, Lou Gehrig had a better batting average than Babe Ruth for the entire season. *How come?*

Answer on page 110

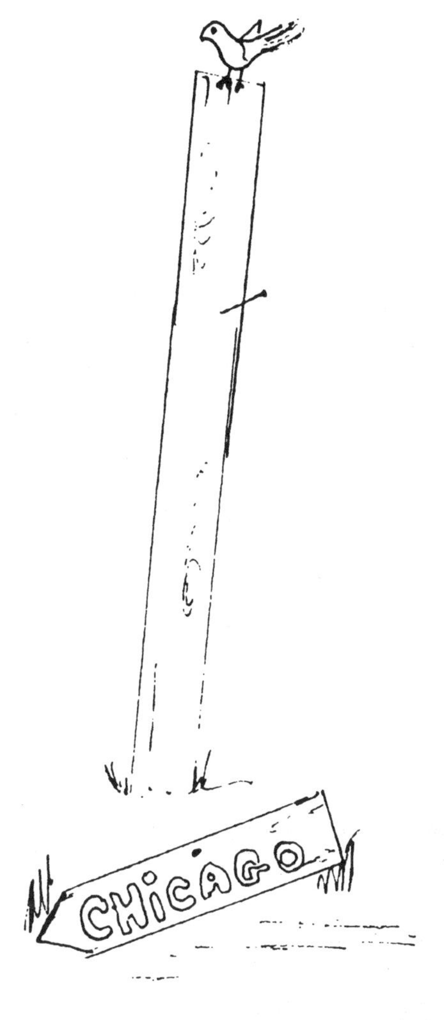

You encounter a man at a fork in the road. One fork leads to Chicago and you want to know which one it is. *What question can you ask so that you will be certain how to get to Chicago regardless of whether the man is a good guy who always tells the truth or a villain who always lies?*

Answer on page 111

90

A man buys a pair of shoes for $10 and gives the owner a $20 bill. Having no change, the owner goes to the barber next door, gets change and gives the customer $10 and the shoes. Later the barber tells him that the $20 bill was counterfeit so the shoe store owner gives the barber $20. If the shoes actually cost the shoe store owner $5, *how much did he lose on the whole affair?*

Answer on page 10

91

Fill in the squares in the following diagram with numbers from 1 to 8 so that no number is adjacent to one that is in sequence with it either horizontally, vertically or diagonally.

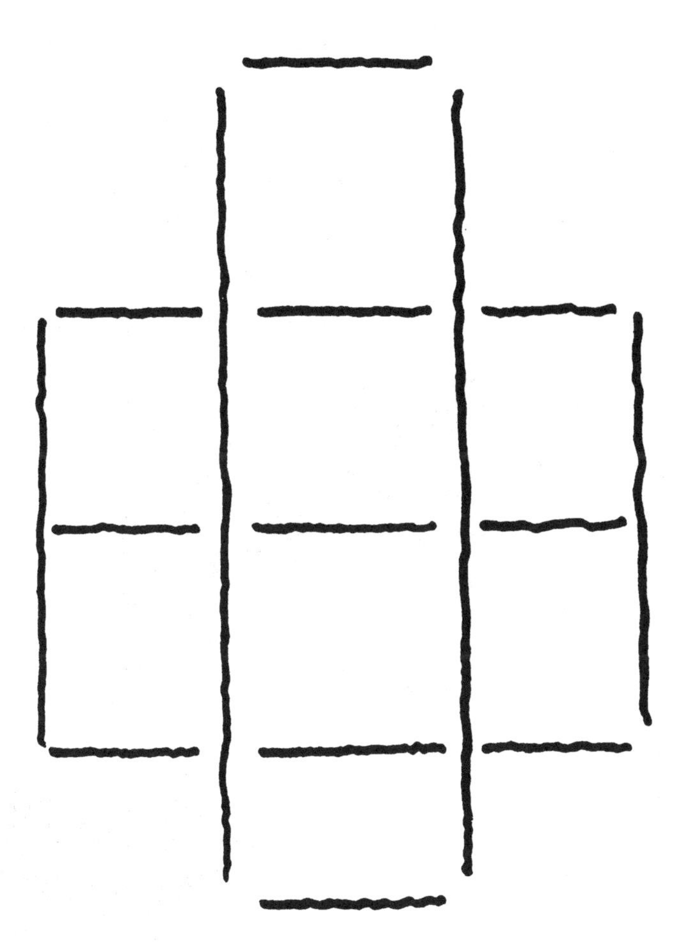

Answer on page 102

92

Jones sold his house for $4,000 and bought it back for $3,500 and sold it again for $4,500. The house is worth the amount he paid for it. *How much did he gain?*

Answer on page 103

93

We have three caskets — a gold, a silver and a lead. There is a prize in one of them. They have statements written on them as follows: On the gold — "The prize is in this casket." On the silver — "The prize is not in this casket." On the lead — "The prize is not in the gold casket." At most, only one statement is true. *Where is the prize?*

Answer on page 104

12 BBs look alike but one is different: either slightly heavier or slightly lighter. *How can you positively identify the odd BB and tell if it is heavier or lighter in the fewest number of weighings on a balance scale?*

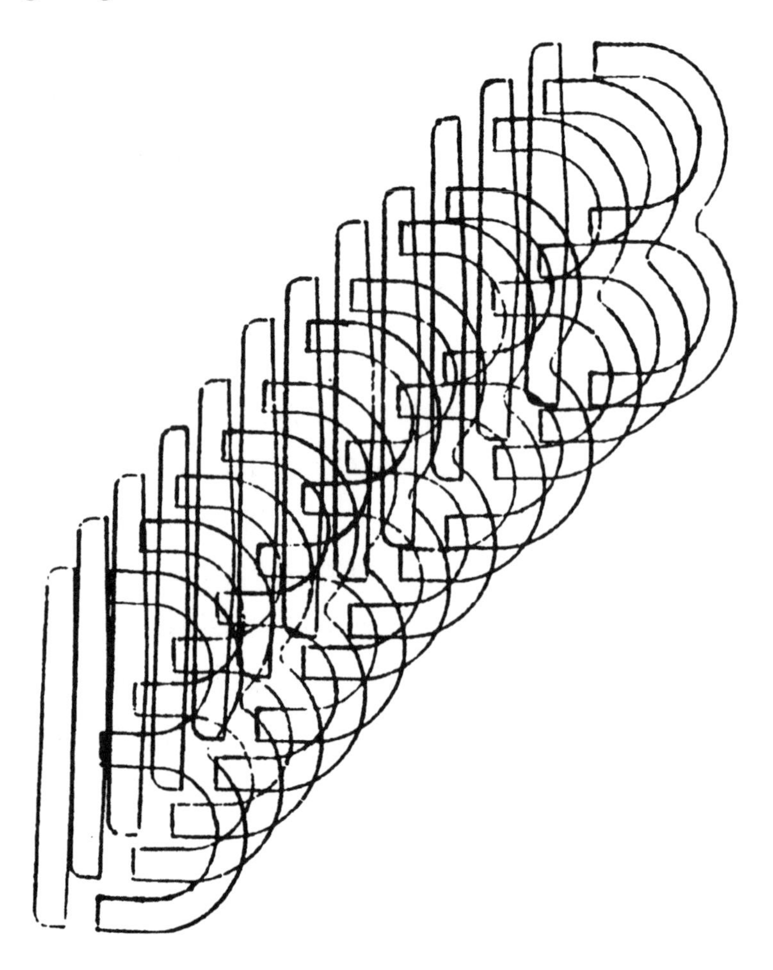

Answer on page 105

An arab sheik died leaving 17 horses to his three sons. His will gave 1/2 to to his oldest son, 1/3 to the middle son and 1/9 to the youngest son. The sons saw the impossibility of doing this, but their uncle came along and suggested a solution that solved their problem. *What was it?*

Answer on page 107

96

Here are the clues to a mathematical crossword puzzle:

ACROSS

1. Half of 6 *across*
5. 3 times 10 *across*
6. See 1 *across*
10. See 5 *across*

DOWN

1. 1st two digits of 1 *across*, times the last two digits
2. Same as 7 *down*
3. Reverse the first two digits of 1 *down* and multiply by 2
4. Reverse the 1st two digits of 1 *across*
7. Same as 2 *down*
8. 2 times a perfect square
9. A perfect square

1	2	3	4
5			
6	7	8	9
10			

Answer on page 108

How many mugs balance a flower pot in the picture below?

Answer on page 109

98

Two mathematicians are walking down the stree
The first says to the second, "I know you have 3 sons. What are their ages?" The second replies, "The product of their ages is 36." The first says, "I can't tell their ages from that." The second says, "Well, the sum of their ages is the same as that address across the street." The first says, "I still can't tell." The second says, "The oldest is visiting his grandfather today." The first says, "Now I know their ages." *Do you?*

Answer on page 109

99

Suppose a 24 foot long wire were added to a band tightly encircling the globe at the equator. *Approximately how much space would there be between the band and the equator everywhere in the world?*

Answer on page 111

100

Here are the clues to a mathematical crossword puzzle:

ACROSS

2. See 6 *down*
5. Square of 4 *down*
7. Twice 5 *across*
9. Same as 6 *down*

DOWN

1. Clue 5 + clue 8 + 200
2. Twice 4 *down*
4. See 5 *across*
6. 3 times 2 *across*
8. see 1 *down*

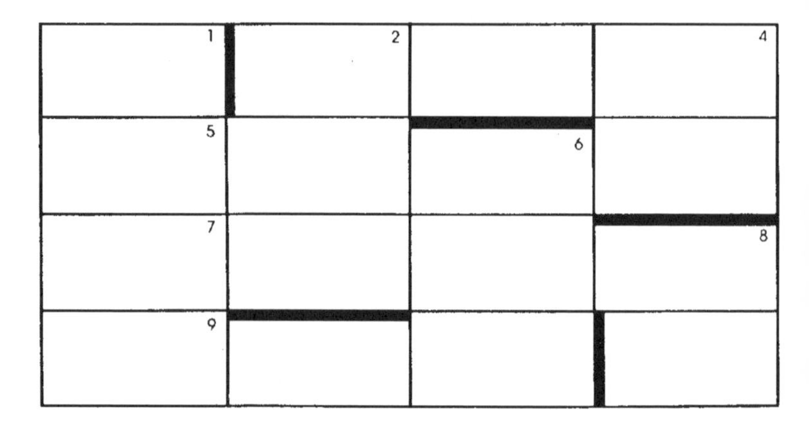

Answer on page 10

Answers

101 Answers

1. The big Indian is the MOTHER of the little Indian!

10. 8. Multiply the preceding two digits.

20. Neither!

30. You have 2 apples.

40. 75 cents. Open all three of once piece and use them to connect the other four pieces to themselves (three connections).

50. Cousin; the only one that is not gender specific.

60.

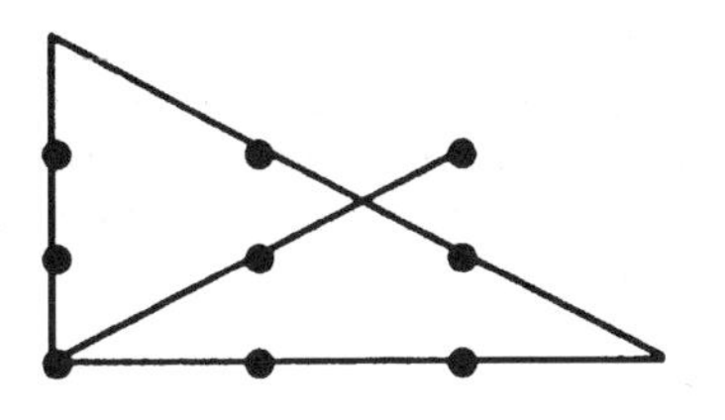

70. It's baseball and he hit a homerun.

80. The body is 20 inches and the tail is 11 inches.

90. $15. The $20 back and forth with the barber cancels out so he simply gave the customer $10 in cash and shoes with had cost him $5.

100.

3 [1]	1 [2]	2	5 [4]
3 [5]	1	3 [6]	6
6 [7]	2	7	2 [8]
3 [9]	7	5	7

2. The letter "n".

11. When you have 1,977 dollars, you have one more dollar than when you have only 1,976 dollars.

21. Never. The boat goes up with the tide.

Answers

31. A. 1001 Arabian Nights
    B. 54 Cards in the Deck (with the Jokers)
    C. 29 Days in February in Leap Year
    D. 24 Hours in a Day
    E. 13 Stripes on the American Flag
    F. 26 Letter of the Alphabet

41. From bag 1 take 1 coin, from bag 2 take 2 coins, from bag 3 take 3 coir and so on through bag 100. When you weigh the coins you have taken they will weigh less than the 5050 ounces they should. The number of quarter ounces the single weighing is short will equal the number of the bag with the bad coins.

51. It's impossible because you cannot come down in zero time. Going up one mile at 30 miles per hour will take two minutes. To average 60 miles per hour for two miles you must do them in two minutes. You've used up all the time going up and therefore would have to come down in nothi flat, an impossible feat.

61.

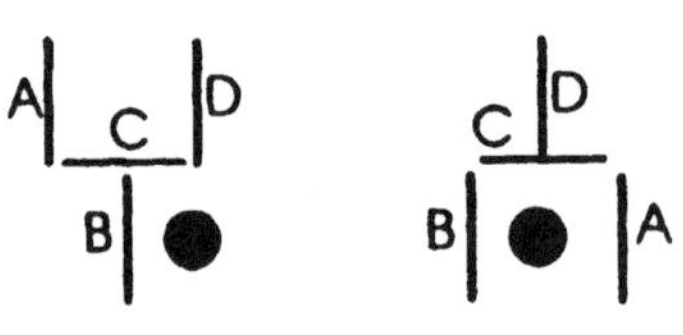

Move A to the new position. Slide C over to join B and the new A.

71. 8,000. Each tire gets 2,000 miles on each wheel.

81. Two days.

91.

	7	
3	1	4
5	8	6
	2	

3. 21. The 16 original, 4 new ones from those 16 butts and 1 more from tho 4 butts.

12. The man is a priest, a rabbi, a preacher, or a judge

103 Answers

22. 9.

32. To the plural noun "princes" add an "s" making the singular noun "princess."

42. The third man is a good guy. The first man will say he's a good guy no matter what he really is – a good guy will say it truthfully, a villain will say it because he always lies. So the second man cannot be telling the truth and the third man is truthfully calling him a liar.

52. The story only accounts for seven men. The man that he put in the last room is number two from the first room – he didn't put the eighth man in any room.

62.

			O				
					O		
O							
				O			
	O						
							O
		O					
						O	

72. The winner knew he had a black mark because he said to himself "If I have a white mark, either of the other two would obviously know that the only way all the hands could go up is if their mark is black. Since neither of them determined the answer quickly, we must all have black marks."

82. Eye, ear, rib, arm, leg, hip, lip, toe, gum, jaw.

92. $1500. He made $500 on the first sale and $1,000 on the second.

4. At 11:59 – after which it doubles and becomes full.

13. Incorrectly.

23. They were a grandfather, father, and son.

Answers

33. "Errers" should be spelled "errors;" "recieve" should be spelled "receive." Those are the only two errors and that's the third error!

43. 100 miles. It takes the trains one hour and twenty minutes to meet. So the bird has flown 100 miles in that time.

53. People in the building like only things with double letters.

63. Four pounds

73. Draw lines connecting the center points of the four sides as shown:

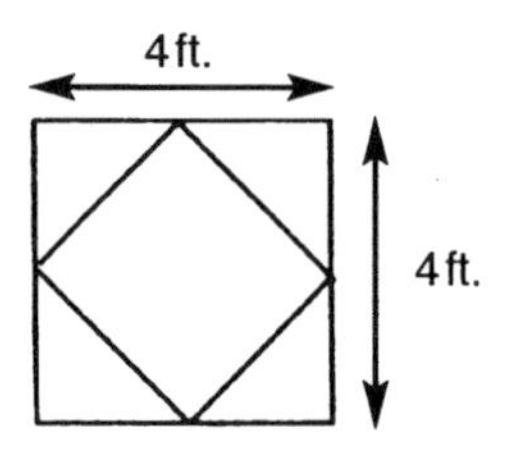

83. 20,000 shoes. 5% of 20,000 people is 1,000 shoes. Half of 19,000 going barefoot is 0 shoes and the other half of 19,000 wearing two shoes each is 19,000 shoes.

93. The silver casket has the prize. The statements on the gold and lead caskets say the opposite so one of them must be true. Since **only** one can be true the statement on the silver casket must be false and therefore contain the prize.

5. He says, "You are going to hang me." They can't hang him because that would mean he **didn't** lie. They can't shoot him because that would mean he didn't tell the truth.

14. Starting with the last stroke of 12:00, 12:15, 12:30, 12:45, 1:00, 1:15, 1:30, 1:45 and the first chime of 2:00.

24. 12.

34. The Prime Minister drew a slip and said, "I'll take the other one." He then showed the judges the one he drew which read "GO." If the King was honest, the other one should say "STAY," and unless the King wanted to show his dishonesty and get caught cheating, the King had to let the Prime Minister stay.

105 Answers

4. One, Two, Three, Four, Five – so S(ix).
Monday, Tuesday, Wednesday, Thursday – so F(riday).
December, November, October, September, August – so J(uly).

4. Take the chicken across. Then take the fox across and bring back the chicken. Then take the grain across and leave it with the fox. Then go back and bring the chicken.

4. 512. $[(13+747+7+9+4) - (24 + 500)] \div 1/2$

4. The neat barber must have given the messy one the bad haircut and the messy one must have given the neat barber his nice haircut.

4. Yes. If there are six birdhouses, there can't be more than five birds in any one house – and there cannot be zero birds in any one house since all must be occupied. Therefore, if the first five houses are filled with 1,2,3,4, and 5 birds, the sixth house must duplicate one of these numbers since it can't have six or more (there are more birdhouses (6) than there are birds in any one house.)

4. First weigh four BBs on one side and four on the other. If the two sides balance, we will call these standard BBs and of course, the odd one is in the other four which we will call suspect BBs.

   a. Place two suspect BBs on side A and a suspect and a standard on side B. If side B goes up, you know that either the suspect one on side B is light or one of the suspects on side A is heavy.
   b. Weigh the two suspects on side A against each other and if one side goes down it has the heavy one. If they balance, the suspect from side B is light.
   c. If in a, above, the two sides of the scale balance, then the one remaining (unweighed) BB is the odd one. Now, for your third weighing, weigh this one against a standard and find out if it is heavy or light.

   If the first weighing does **not** balance, label the four on the heavy side w, x, y, and z. Label the four on the light side a, b, c, and d. Take y and z from the heavy side and d from the light side—place these on the left. On the right side, place w and x from the heavy side and c from the light side.

(continued on next page)

94. (continued from previous page)

a. If they balance, you know that one of the two remaining from the light side (a & b) is, indeed, light. Weigh them against each other and the side that goes up has the odd, light BB.
b. If they do **not** balance and the right side goes down, you know that either w or x is heavy or d (on the other side) is light.
c. Weigh w and x against each other and if one side goes down, it has the odd, heavy BB. If they balance it shows that d is light.
d. Again, if they do **not** balance but the **left** side goes down, either y or z is heavy or c (on the other side) is light.
e. In that case, weigh y and z against each other and if one side goes down, it has the odd, heavy BB. If they balance, it shows that c is light.

6. It is a picture of his son.

15. No! in 47 BC, they didn't know about BC. It's a fake.

25. Did you say "THE" twice?

35. Once. Take a marble from the box labeled "Black & White." If it's black, then it must contain **two** blacks. Since the one labeled "Two Whites" **cannot have** two whites or two blacks, it must contain a black and a white. Then, of course, the one labeled "Two Blacks" must have the two whites. Likewise if the original marble is white.

45. 16 days. After 15 days, he's fifteen feet up, 5 feet from the top. On the 16th day, his five foot jump takes him out and he doesn't hit the wall and fall back.

55. The answer is not 4 inches! The answer is 2 inches. Starting at page 1 of Volume 1, he misses the first cover and pages of the first book because of the way books stand on a shelf. So he goes through the last cover of Volume 1, the two covers and pages of Volume 2, and the back cover of Volume 3.

107
Answers

5. Ray Brown, the professor, charged $5
Gail Jones, the lawyer, charged $10
Ben Smith, the doctor, charged $15

5. "One, two, three, etc." The numbers from one to one hundred have no "a" in them.

5. Pull B down, back up and pull A down – giving BEA. Leave B behind and push A up into X-Y. Go around and pull A all the way down. Then back up giving BAE. Go forward and back B up into X-Y. Back up and pull B down to desired new position – AEB. Go forward and back A up into desired position.

5. To solve their problem, the uncle lent them a horse, making the total 18 horses. The oldest took 1/2 = 9; the middle son took 1/3 = 6; the youngest son took 1/9 = 2. That adds up to 17 so they gave the uncle back his horse and everyone ended up happy.

. He said, "Can I buy a pair of scissors?"

6. A man couldn't possibly marry his widow's sister anywhere because if his wife is a widow, he is dead!

6. Not at all.

6. In any single elimination tournament, every player loses once except the winner. Thus, there are one less matches than the number of players.
a) 99 matches
b) 1,499 matches
c) 147,689 matches

6. Ten times. The minute hand does not cross the hour hand in the first hour or the last hour.

6. There is no other dollar! The men spent $27. $25 went for the room and the other two were kept by the bellboy.

6. The batter hit a home-run which tied the game, making the score 3-3, so the final score has to be at least 4-3. Baseball cannot end in a tie.

6. Start both hourglasses. When the four minute glass runs out, turn it over (4 minutes elapsed). When the seven minute glass runs out, turn it over (7 minutes elapsed). When the four minute glass runs out this time (8 minutes elapsed), the seven minute glass has been running for 1 minute. Turn it over once again. When it stops, nine minutes have elapsed.

Answers

86. Throw it straight up in the air. It will stop and then come down.

96.

[1] 3	[2] 9	[3] 8	[4] 9
[5] 4	5	6	3
[6] 7	[7] 9	[8] 7	[9] 8
[10] 1	5	2	1

8. One **is** a nickel!

17. There is not **any** dirt in a hole.

27. When they **meet** they are both the same distance from Chicago.

37. Three. At worst, the first two will be a black and a white so the third one is bound to make a pair.

47. She is walking.

57. The first man is a villain and the second man is a good guy. Since the first man must have answered yes in any case, (truthfully if he's a good guy and lying, if he's a villain) the second one is telling the truth so he's a good guy and the first man is a villain .

67.
1. The health **SPA IN** the travel folder looked attractive.
2. Water was rationed so each got a small **CAN A DA**y.
3. Elv**IRA Q**uestioned the monthly electric bill.
4. Swoll**EN GLAND**s can be very painful.
5. We had to wait for sup**PER U**ntil the guests arrived.
6. Shou**T, "HAIL," AND** be recognized.
7. You're a **ROMAN, I A**ssume.
8. Ye**S, WE DEN**y all of the charges, judge.

77. Thursday. The only days Mr. A can say "I lied yesterday" are Mondays (lying) and Thursdays (truthfully). The only days Mr. B can say "I lied yesterday" are Thursdays (lying) and Sundays (truthfully). So the only day they can both say it is Thursday.

87. Three. A,B and C take off together. After 1/8 of the distance, (which uses 1/4 of a tank) C transfers 1/4 to A and 1/4 to B. C then has 1/4 left to get safely home.

A & B continue another 1/8 of the way (using another 1/4 tank each). B transfers 1/4 to A leaving himself 1/2 a tankful which gets him safely home.

A, now with a full tank, continues to the 3/4 point where, with an empty tank, he is met by C who gives him 1/4 of a tankful. They now continue to the 7/8 point (another 1/8 of the way) where they both run out of gas but they are met by plane B which gives each of them 1/4 and they all head home safely, arriving there with all of them empty.

97.
a. 1 mug + 1 pot = 1 cat
b. 2 mugs + 1 corn = 1 cat (combining pictures 1 & 2)
c. 1 1/2 corns = 1 cat (from picture 3)
d. 2 mugs = 1/2 corn (2 mugs + 1 corn = 1 1/2 corns from b & c above)
e. 6 mugs = 1 cat (from d, 4 mugs =1 corn so b could be written 2 mugs + 4 mugs = 1 cat)
f. 1 mug + 1 pot = 6 mugs (from a)
g. Therefore 1 pot = 5 mugs.

9. The advice was "Trade horses"

18. Eleven. Every month but February has 30 days.

28. Two sons go across, one comes back. The father goes across and the other son comes back. Then the two sons go across.

38. 30 minutes. First do steaks 1 and 2 on their A side taking 10 minutes. Then steak 3 on its A side with steak 1 on its B side taking 10 minutes. Then steaks 2 and 3 on their B sides taking 10 minutes – a total of 30 minutes.

98. 2-2-9. There are only 8 combinations of three numbers that multiply out to 36. 6 of their sums are unique so if it were one of those the first mathematician would recognize the number across street that matches and he would know the answer, but he doesn't. Two combinations result in the same sum so he can't know which is correct. Upon hearing that there **is** an "oldest" he sees that only one of the two sums qualifies, because the other doesn't have an oldest child.

19. 9.

Answers

48. Jake should fire into the air.
    a. If Jake hits Max, Alex will kill Jake on his first shot so Jake's chances are 0.
    b. If Jake hits Alex, Max will kill Jake 2 out of 3 times. If he misses, Jake will shoot at Max and probably miss - giving Max more chances to kill him. So Jake's chances are <u>less</u> than 1/3.
    c. If Jake hits no one, Max will certainly not shoot at him so either Max hits Alex or Max hits no one.
        1) If Max hits Alex, Jake will shoot at Max and has a 1/3 chance of killing him. If Jake misses, Max may miss him too, so Jake may get another chance. So Jake's chances are <u>greater</u> than 1/3.
        2) If Max misses Alex, Alex will then kill Max. Jake will then have one shot at Alex after which, if he misses, Alex will kill him. Jakes chances are 1/3.

58. Impossible! There will always be a half-distance left

68. Weigh three BBs on each side. If one side goes down it must contain the heavy BB. Weigh two of those, one on each side and if one side goes down, it must contain the heavy BB. If they balance, then the one you did not weigh is the heavy BB. If, on the first weighing, the scale balances, then you have two BBs left. Place one on each side, the heavy one will go down.

78. In order to measure exactly 45 minutes, light Rope A on both ends and Rope B on one end. When Rope A is totally burned out, a half-hour will have elapsed. At this time, light the other end of Rope B. When B is extinguished, it will be 15 after A burned out, thus 45 minutes total. Even though the ropes do not burn at a constant rate, lighting on both ends will make it burn out in half the time.

88. Here is an example of how this seemingly impossibility is possible. Ruth batted .300 for 200 times at bat the first half of the season (60 hits) and .400 for 100 times at bat during the second half of the season (40 hits) – a total of 100 hits for 300 times at bat so his average was .333.

    Gehrig batted .290 (less than Ruth's .300) for 100 times at bat the first half of the season (29 hits) and .390 (less than Ruth's .400) for 200 times at bat during the second half of the season (78 hits) – a total of 107 hits for 300 times at bat. Thus, Gehrig's average was .357 and therefore greater than Ruth's .333.

29. The bottle costs $102.50 and the cork $2.50.

39. Twice. Cut one segment for the first night. Cut two segments for the second night taking back the first one in change. Use that one for the third night. On the forth night give the remaining four-segment piece taking back the one and the two in change. The fifth night give the one. The sixth night give the two and take the one back as change. The seventh night give the one.

49. 20. There is one for each of ten groups of ten plus ten extra for the 90 group.

59. Zero. If three are correct, the fourth must be correct.

69. The trains come one minute apart. For example, the north bound train comes at 9:00 AM and the south bound at 9:01. So nine minutes out of ten, the north bound is the first to come along.

79. #1 must be a villain because if his statement were true, he would be a truth-telling villain and there is no such thing. So his statement is false and there must be at least one good guy. If #2 is a villain, then #3 would be the good guy – and so #2's statement would be true – so he can't be a villain and must be a good guy. Since his statement, then, is true (only one good guy), #3 must be a villain.

89. "If I ask you whether this road (pointing to one) goes to Chicago, what would you say?" If it does, the good guy says, "Yes." And the villain would really say "No" (lying) but now he lies about what he would say so he answers "Yes." Similar reasoning if the road does not go to chicago in which case they would both say, "NO."

99. The difference in the circumference = 24 feet
The formula for the circumference of a circle is $2\Pi r$
$2\Pi r_2 - 2\Pi r_1 = 24$ feet
$2\Pi (r_2 - r_1) = 24$ feet
$r_2 - r_1 = 24/2\Pi = 24/6.28 = 3.82$ feet
The new radius is almost 4 feet longer and therefore the band will be about four feet away from the surface.